Reality check

Melissa Jemison

BookLeaf Publishing

India | USA | UK

Presentation by *BookLeaf Publishing*

Web: www.bookleafpub.com

E-mail: info@bookleafpub.com

ISBN: 9789363314993

First edition 2024

PREFACE

Trauma. Healing. Spirituality. Transformation. Embracing the dark night of the soul to be reborn again.

A helpless child

I just want to cry to let it all out, to punch something, break something, to scream and shout.

So overwhelmed, so angry, so tired.
Why does life take, take, take and drain you inside out?

My heart hurts. My head hurts. A constant battle between love and logic.

To accept any form of love because that's what
my heart desires.

Toxicity, narcissism, manipulation, and
gaslighting.
Telling myself, "No, they love me. I'm the
problem."

A child with no mother, no father, no siblings,
no friends.
Left to face the world with zero guidance.

No clothes, no food, nowhere safe to sleep.
Abused, molested, and verbally mistreated.
Painting a smile on my face, wasn't the best
escape. Just got better at hiding the pain.

Became addicted to sex, love, and money,
suppressing the demons in my brain.

A temporary fix at best, to numb the rest. I
wanted to end it all.
The dumbest shit I could've ever wished for, as a
child, was to be an adult.

Sorry Means Nothing

Don't tell me you're Sorry
Because you couldn't love me properly
That sorrow and regret
Something I'd never forget
How you begged me to stay and promised to
change
The change I prayed for
The change I craved, for a family I couldn't save

Don't tell me you're Sorry, for blatant disrespect
The child I bared for you, I raised alone
He said "Daddy don't love me"
I bowed my head. Ashamed.
This was the man I loved. The person I chose, to
let me down, to make me grow

Don't tell me you're Sorry
I have no sympathy for the time wasted
The nights I cried, the bruises made, the wounds
you created

Don't tell me you're Sorry when you see me
happy
I rebuilt myself after the pain and misery
Soul tie released, you owe me nothing

Another man's trash is another man's treasure
Our child will grow to remember the love from
his mother
All the sorries in the world could never make me
forget, how low and depressed you made me
reflect
I prayed to grow and love myself more
I vowed to never let a man have control
My emotions so deep, a heart so strong
I pray those evil ways will spare our son.

Lucky Love

5

How'd I get so lucky? I love you so much. I
crave your heart, your affection, your touch.

It's deeper than looks, it's deeper than lust.
Whenever I'm around you, I can't get enough.

Your energy unmatched, your heart so pure.
Your love so compelling, simply so rare.

No lies and deceit, not afraid to be me.
A masculine man unleashed my femininity.

Vulnerable. Open to love.
Past the hurt. I'm ready to trust.

Trust that he's my person.
God sent him to me.
It's time to let go, let him take the lead.

I prayed for this.
A life so rich, of peace and bliss.

No idea what tomorrow will bring, taking slow
strides. We've just met, yet so intertwined.

So familiar, so uncanny. He says love at first sight. My other half, maybe my soulmate from another life.

Is this the honeymoon stage? A spark so intense. Time stands still by the touch of his lips.

Living in the present. I hope it never ends. When our time's up, I pray we meet again.

Bpd

This continuous feeling of emptiness
Like I'm not good enough
I feel so lonely
Even with someone I love
Really high highs and awfully low lows
Depressed, isolated, and spiraling outta control
I'm beautiful today and hate myself tomorrow
How can someone so pretty carry so much
sorrow
They see all the smiles and laughter
Hiding my pain and trauma
I hate talking about my problems
I don't wanna burden them with my drama

Feeling hopeless, carrying this physically
emotional pain
Therapists told me there's a chemical imbalance
in my brain
Borderline Personality Disorder in a constant
fight-or-flight mode
Abandoned, insecure, and afraid to get close
Exhausted and stuck
I dream of closing my eyes and never waking
up.

What would you choose?

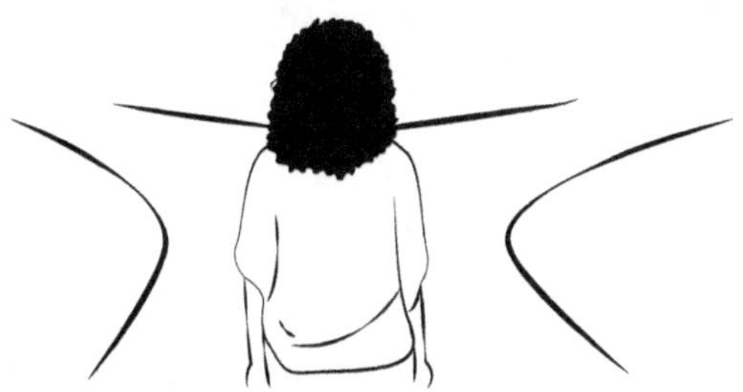

In fight-or-flight mode
It's time for me to go
I have to choose myself
I gave so much of myself to everyone else, to
remain broken shattered and lost
Stuck in a limbo, my soul searching for an exit
Mental retreat, soul screaming for peace
A Trauma release, suppressed emotions relieved
When am I gonna be happy with me?
If gone tomorrow, would you be happy with the
life you led?
If you had the chance, would you choose a
different life instead?
The grass ain't always greener on the side you
choose
There's always someone with a worse life than
you
So what would change? Would you still take the
path? Camus said, "You will never live if you
are always looking for the meaning of life."

Barely holding on

Don't drag me down. I refuse to drown
Waves crashing high, why am I alive?
Running from my problems, in need of escape
Not feeling protected, secure, or safe
Barely holding on..
On my last breath, before I blow up and do
something I regret
The calm before the storm
Don't take it for weakness
I gave you the benefit of the doubt
Now I'm looking stupid

Flipped my switch, I'm ready to kill
Fuck being nice, you wanted this side
Deep down in my mind, I can see, every
scenario that takes my freedom from me
So I tuck it away and run like hell
I can't give in and give my soul to the devil
I'm good at running and hiding the pain but no
matter what…
I have to face my demons again.

Unexpected

I think about you all day
I see you when I close my eyes
Those strong dark arms with tattoos you can
barely see
Those big soft lips that kiss me so sensually
Tall and firm
Yet affectionate and gentle
This is a man I just can't get off my mental
I daydream about being together forever
Puppy dog love
Honeymoon stage
Is he a lesson or a blessing?
What about fate?
His soul intertwined with mine
Is this a sign? He feels so familiar
Like I've known him my whole life
I feel at home
His hug and kiss
I yearn for more
Maybe marriage and kids
But what happens when things get tough?
Will he push me away or embrace me with love?
This consuming fear of whether it will last
My heart tender with fear from the past
Unexpectedly falling for him
How did this happen? How will it end?

Home

Home sweet home
This bittersweet feeling
The smell of Momma's cooking
My 8-pound pomeranian barking as I near the
door
You don't realize what you have 'til it's gone is
the truest statement
I've never known,
How welcoming it is to be held in my mother's
arms
A hug welcome back home
You've been gone too long
I had to clear my head
I had to run away
Escape my stress and process the betrayal
I can't deny I'm still like a baby waiting for my
mom to soothe me when I cry
I've prayed for the days

To see my family's face
To be accepted and feel loved
To be supported and have trust
Even dysfunctional and fucked up
To have my back through it all
To feel safe, let down this wall
No judgement, no disgrace
To see my momma's face
When I walked through that door
Home is where the heart is
And I value it that much more
Home sweet home.

Dickmatized

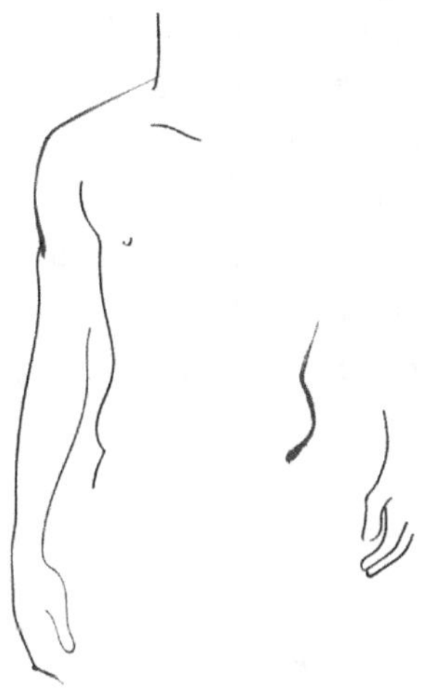

Kissing on my lips, my breasts, my neck
Whispering in my ear, "This is your dick"
Opening my legs, my pussy lips salivate.
Gently tasting my juices, playing with my clit,
as your tongue swirls, and my body gets tense
Begging for you inside of me
I'm moaning and screaming, "Daddy please!"
He enters so slowly, such nice deep strokes
Looking me in my eyes as his hand grabs my
throat
Harder and harder, my eyes roll back
In deep awe, as I climax

Flipping me over on my hands and knees
pounding my pussy, smacking my cheeks
Left and right, feeling my walls
Infatuated, enticed, draining his balls
Cumming in my pussy
Sweet cream pie
Dripping down my legs, coating my thighs
Damn I love him
He has me so dickmatized.

Acceptance

I accept all your flaws
I accept the good with the bad
All your imperfections, your baggage, and your
bad habits

I know you get angry
I know you gotta be in control
But I'm a reflection of you, I'm just as capable
I won't let you fall
I can carry the weight
Whatever burden we carry, I promise I won't
break

I accept when you're depressed
I accept when you cry
I accept when you're at your worst
I'm always on your side
I'm gonna ride until we die

I'm not perfect, I'm healing too
If you don't judge me, I won't judge you
My love is genuine
My love is nurturing
My love is unconditional

Whatever hand you deal me
I won't run away
Just accept me how I accept you
The ugly, the success, even the bittersweet
I'm here to stay.

What's the point

What's the point in living?
Working paycheck to paycheck
Working to pay for land God made
Having to look over your back, barely surviving
every day

What's the point in living?
Getting married,
Reproducing children,
Just to raise them, get sick, or die of old age

What's the point in living?
All the responsibilities
All of the stress
All the fake love and challenging ass tests

What is after this? Do we live again?
Is there another life for our souls?
Is this hell on earth? What's the damn goal?

Blame myself

Body tired, begging for comfort, begging for rest
and change
Being a people person and being let down every
chance

Being in love, with the idea of love
Willing to accept anything, to cope with the
childhood trauma of not being enough
Giving someone too much control over your
thoughts and emotions
Mind running down a rabbit hole, if only you
could give yourself that same devotion

When you've been put down and dragged
through the mud by someone you love
The lies and deceit, building a wall limiting your
trust
Afraid to hurt again
Afraid to let someone in

Ready to run, start over, leave everyone behind
But what would it solve? You still can't escape
your mind
Being stuck in your head, an unfathomable pain
The truth hurts the most but you're the one to
blame.

Bam!

Just when I thought things couldn't get any
worse, it hits me.
Bam!
No, literally. A freaking car hits me and knocks
me on the ground. I'm scraped up, body aching,
chest pounding.
Panic attack.
Everything goes black.
Why is this happening to me?
There's no such thing as a coincidence.
Everything is meant to be.
Skrrrttt.
Someone helped me up.
"God bless you. Are you okay?"
All I could think is, let me call my mom and tell
her I am safe.
Body shocked, adrenaline pumping, the police
on the way.
Strangers staring. Watching in dismay.
Put me on a gurney, in the ambulance I go.
I know he hit me by accident, but it's out of his
control.
Grateful I'm not paralyzed and get to go home to
my son. I couldn't imagine being on my
deathbed. I've barely lived. I'm way too young.

The only thought that crosses your mind in this
sort of unfortunate event, is that I need to start
living everyday like it's my last. You never know
when your life will flash before your eyes.
Later that day, I see my son's smile. Boy am I
glad, that God be watching out.

My love

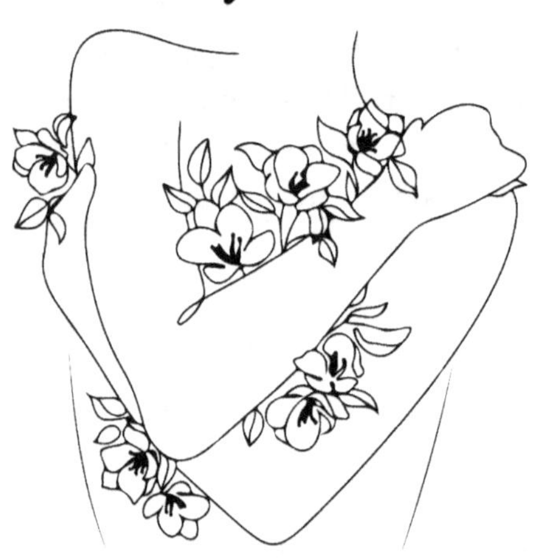

You can fuck whoever you wanna fuck, be with whoever you want, but in the back of your mind, you will always think of me.
I'm more than a pretty face, nice ass, and cute smile. I loved you unconditionally and bore your child. I blessed you with my presence and my nurturing soul. I gave you motivation and I pushed you to grow. I cheered you on when you succeeded. After a long day, I cooked a hot meal for you to eat. I picked up your slack, when you weren't feeling well. I helped piece you back together when you didn't feel yourself. I helped you provide when you didn't have enough. I even fought aside you, when things got rough. When your friends turned their back, I stayed

through it all. You cried on my shoulders, when
your back was against the wall. When your
family didn't check on you, my family took you
in. I gave you all of me and I still wouldn't
change a thing. I learned a valuable lesson from
my experience with you. Love yourself more so
the expectations of their love won't hinder you.

Easier said than done

It's easier to be mad and guard my heart than to
keep going back to you.
It's easier to be miserable and cry myself to sleep
than to torture myself with what could be
It's easier to let go than to keep trying to make it
work and failing time and time again
It's easier to run away than to be stuck in my
feelings
It's hard seeing you turn your back on me
It's hard seeing you move on and be happy
It's hard walking away from the years we've had
It's hard letting go of the idea of a happy family
It's easier to argue than to work things out
It's easier to shut down and not work on yourself
It's easier to numb the pain to stay out your head
It's hard to accept that everything is done
It's hard to accept being alone
It's hard to accept the truth when it hurts
The truth is that no matter what my mind tells
me, I still want it to work.

Cupcake

Furry. Golden. 8 pounds max. Toy pomeranian. Bark but no bite. Loyal and observant. Great watchdog. Loves people and kids. Met her when she was 6 weeks old and her tail wagged. She leaped with joy. I held her in my hands. So tiny. She licked my palm. I knew I wanted to take her home. She chose me. She never barked. Quiet as a mouse. With loving and big black eyes. She knows when I'm sad. She knows when I'm sick. She grew as I had my first child. Experienced everything with me. Ate any food she could get her paws on. She'd wait 'til you turned your head to snatch your pizza from your hand. Now she's getting old and sick. I see her pain and I feel sad. I hate how painful it is to watch her grow old. I hate thinking of her death. I've become so attached to her. My spirit animal. My best friend. My emotional support dog. I love my Cupcake.

Run

Ran away from home
Ran away from school
Ran away from foster care
Ran away from my past
Ran away from the job that didn't appreciate me
Ran away from my hometown
Ran away from people who abused me
Ran away from everything that didn't align
Ran away from my feelings
Ran away from the hurt
Ran away from the truth
Ran away from love
Ran away from responsibilities
Ran away from life itself
When things got tough I ran and didn't look back
My inner child told me it was no longer safe and
it was time to go
But no matter how much you run
You can never escape the pain you carry
The memories you hold
It doesn't go away
The problems just grow

Society

Clear blue sky, dark at night
Dozens of white clouds, with not a star in sight
Cars driving by, headlights beaming, horns
honking, kids screaming
A city that never sleeps,
Diverse and cultured
Poverty, middle class, and the rich—all with the
same problems, the same schemes, the same
trauma
We're all human
We all bleed
The adolescent innocent
The adults as crooked as they come
Food prices high, everybody scraping crumbs
Takes a village to raise our children
We're losing to the streets
Less fatherly figures, more mothers crying
themselves to sleep
Family secrets, bigger wounds to hide
Mental illnesses high, kids committing suicide
Black-on-black crime, no wonder the white
survive

They taught us false narratives to keep us
ignorant and blind
Stuck in a cycle only the awakened realize
They called it a pandemic, it's just modern
genocide
To them a life is just another sacrifice
Demonic beings walk among you and I
Always protect your energy because darkness
needs the light